FINGERPICKING Disney

ISBN 978-0-634-09888-8

**Walt Disney Music Company
Wonderland Music Company, Inc.**

DISTRIBUTED BY

HAL•LEONARD®
CORPORATION

7777 W. BLUEMOUND RD. P.O. BOX 13819 MILWAUKEE, WI 53213

In Australia Contact:
Hal Leonard Australia Pty. Ltd.
4 Lentara Court
Cheltenham, Victoria, 3192 Australia
Email: ausadmin@halleonard.com

Visit Hal Leonard Online at
www.halleonard.com

INTRODUCTION TO FINGERSTYLE GUITAR

Fingerstyle (a.k.a. fingerpicking) is a guitar technique that means you literally pick the strings with your right-hand fingers and thumb. This contrasts with the conventional technique of strumming and playing single notes with a pick (a.k.a. flatpicking). For fingerpicking, you can use any type of guitar: acoustic steel-string, nylon-string classical, or electric.

THE RIGHT HAND

The most common right-hand position is shown below:

Use a high wrist; arch your palm as if you were holding a ping-pong ball. Keep the thumb outside and away from the fingers, and let the fingers do the work rather than lifting your whole hand.

The thumb generally plucks the bottom strings with downstrokes on the left side of the thumb and thumbnail. The other fingers pluck the higher strings using upstrokes with the fleshy tip of the fingers and fingernails. The thumb and fingers should pluck one string per stroke and not brush over several strings.

Another picking option you may choose to use is called **hybrid picking** (a.k.a. plectrum-style fingerpicking). Here, the pick is usually held between the thumb and first finger, and the three remaining fingers are assigned to pluck the higher strings.

THE LEFT HAND

The left-hand fingers are numbered 1 through 4:

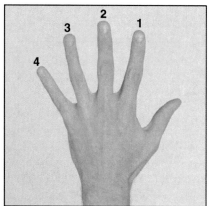

Be sure to keep your fingers arched, with each joint bent; if they flatten out across the strings, they will deaden the sound when you fingerpick. As a general rule, let the strings ring as long as possible when playing fingerstyle.

The Bare Necessities

from Walt Disney's THE JUNGLE BOOK

Words and Music by Terry Gilkyson

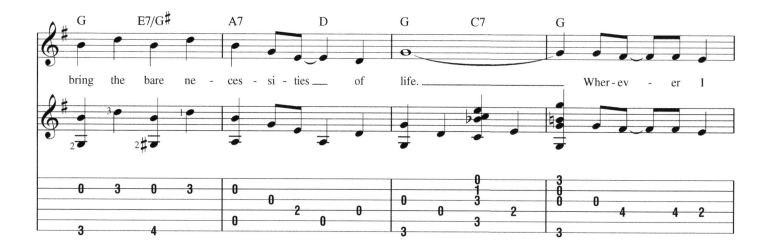

bring the bare ne - ces - si - ties ___ of life. _____ Wher - ev - er I

wan - der, _____ wher - ev - er I roam, _____ I could - n't be

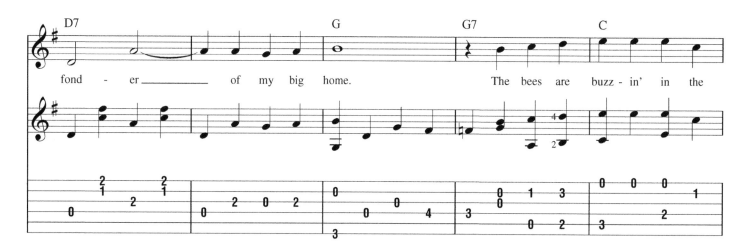

fond - er _____ of my big home. The bees are buzz - in' in the

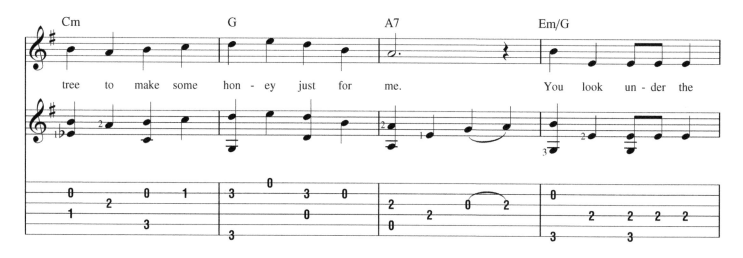

tree to make some hon - ey just for me. You look un - der the

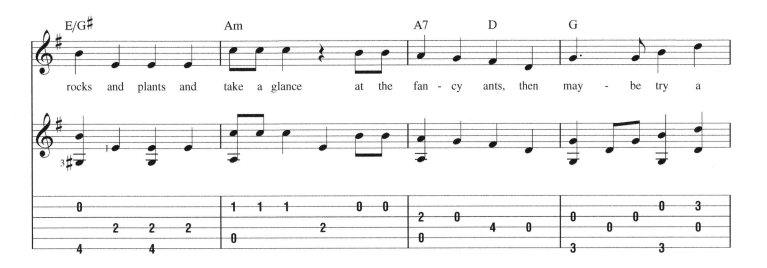

Additional Lyrics

2. Look for the bare necessities, the simple bare necessities;
Forget about your worries and your strife.
I mean the bare necessities, that's why a bear can rest at ease
With just the bare necessities of life.
When you pick a paw-paw or prickly pear,
And you prick a raw paw next time beware.
Don't pick the prickly pear by paw,
When you pick a pear, try to use the claw.
But you don't need to use the claw
When you pick a pear of the big paw-paw,
Have I given you a clue?
The bare necessities of life will come to you, they'll come to you!

3. Look for the bare necessities, the simple bare necessities;
Forget about your worries and your strife.
I mean the bare necessities, or Mother Nature's recipes
That brings the bare necessities of life.
So just try to relax (Oh, yeah!) in my back yard,
If you act like that bee acts you're workin' too hard.
Don't spend your time just lookin' around
For something you want that can't be found.
When you find out you can life without it
And go along not thinkin' about it.
I'll tell you something true.
The bare necessities of life will come to you, they'll come to you!

Be Our Guest

from Walt Disney's BEAUTY AND THE BEAST

Lyrics by Howard Ashman
Music by Alan Menken

Drop D tuning:
(low to high) D–A–D–G–B–E

℀ **Chorus**

Moderately

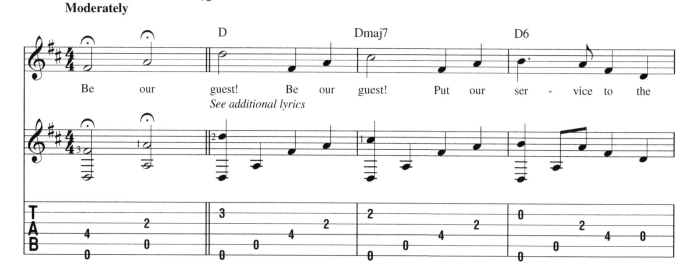

Be our guest! Be our guest! Put our ser - vice to the

See additional lyrics

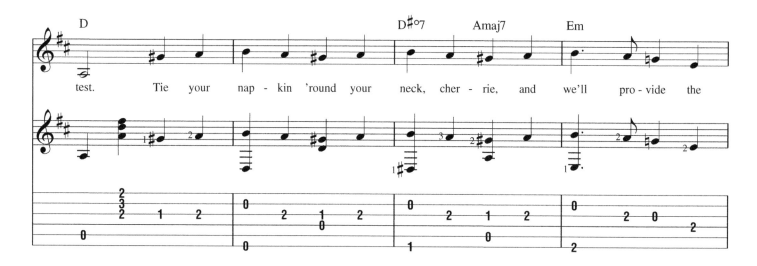

test. Tie your nap - kin 'round your neck, cher - rie, and we'll pro - vide the

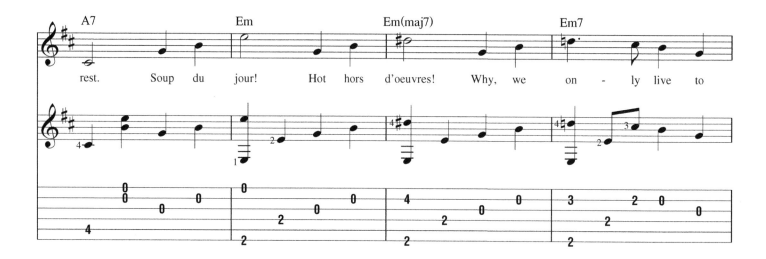

rest. Soup du jour! Hot hors d'oeuvres! Why, we on - ly live to

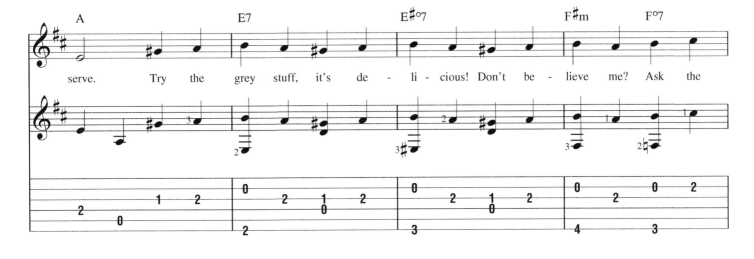

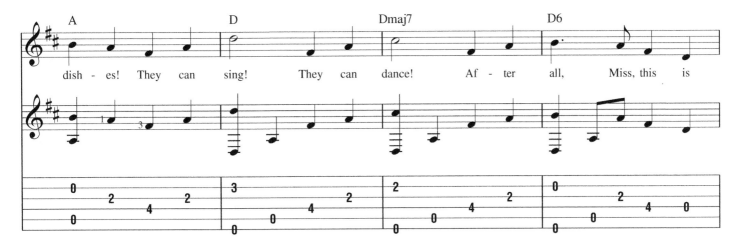

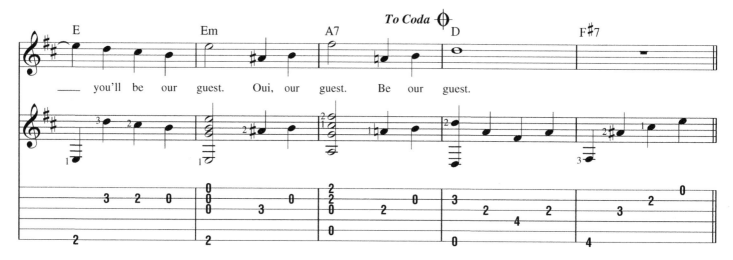

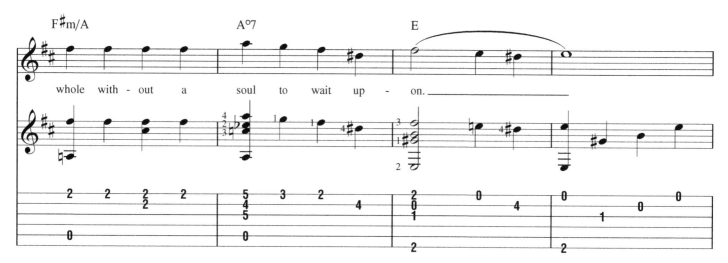

Additional Lyrics

2. Ten years we've been rusting, needing so much more than dusting.
   Needing exercise, a chance to use our skill!
   Most days we just sit around the castle, flabby, fat and lazy.
   You walked in and whoops-a-daisy!

Chorus It's a guest! It's a guest! Sakes alive, well, I'll be blessed!
   Wine's been poured and thank the Lord, I've had the napkins freshly pressed.
   With dessert she'll want tea. And my dear, that's fine with me.
   While the cups do their soft shoeing, I'll be bubbling! I'll be brewing!
   I'll get warm, piping hot! Heaven's sakes! Is that a spot?
   Clean it up! We want our company impressed.
   We've got a lot do do. Is it one lump or two, for you, our guest?
   Be our guest! Be our guest!

Beauty and the Beast

from Walt Disney's BEAUTY AND THE BEAST

Lyrics by Howard Ashman
Music by Alan Menken

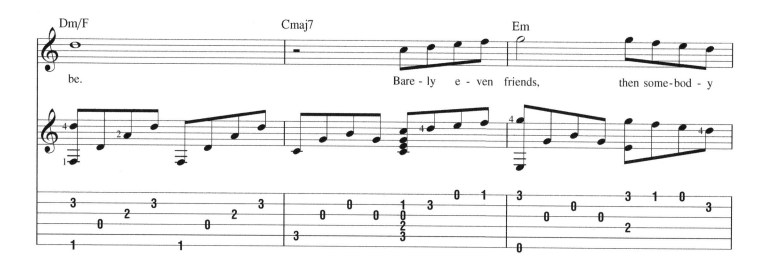

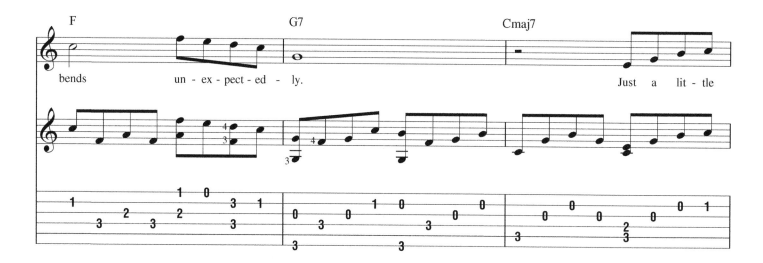

Ev-er as be-fore, ev-er just as sure as the sun will

D.C. al Coda

$\oplus$ **Coda**

rise.

Tale as old as

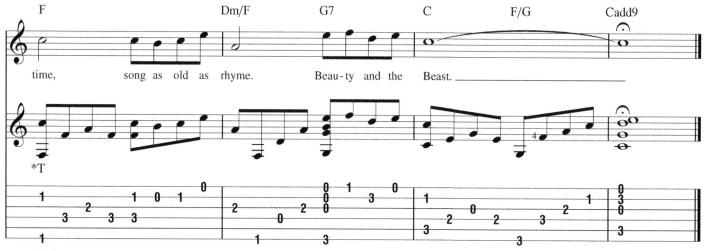

time, song as old as rhyme. Beau-ty and the Beast. _____

*T=Thumb on 6th string. (Or barre chord)

Additional Lyrics

2. Tale as old as time,
   Tune as old as song.
   Bittersweet and strange, finding you can change,
   Learning you were wrong.
   Certain as the sun
   Rising in the east,
   Tale as old as time, song as old as rhyme.
   Beauty and the Beast.
   Tale as old as time, song as old as rhyme.
   Beauty and the Beast.

Can You Feel the Love Tonight

from Walt Disney Pictures' THE LION KING

Music by Elton John
Lyrics by Tim Rice

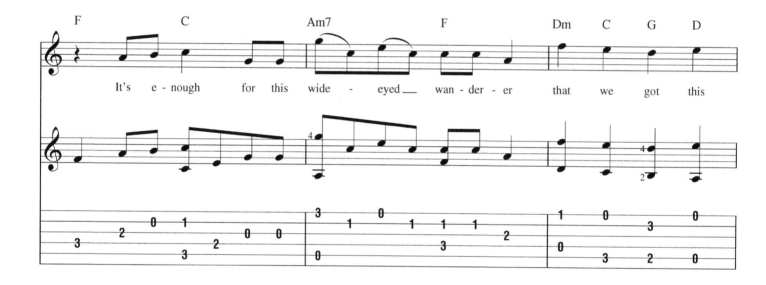

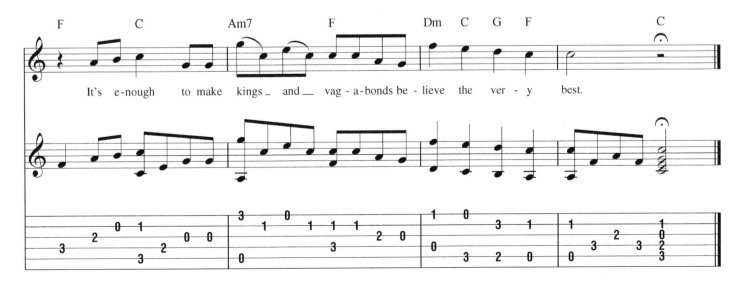

Candle on the Water

from Walt Disney's PETE'S DRAGON

Words and Music by Al Kasha and Joel Hirschhorn

1. I'll be your can-dle on the wa-ter,   my love for you will al-ways
2., 3. *See additional lyrics*

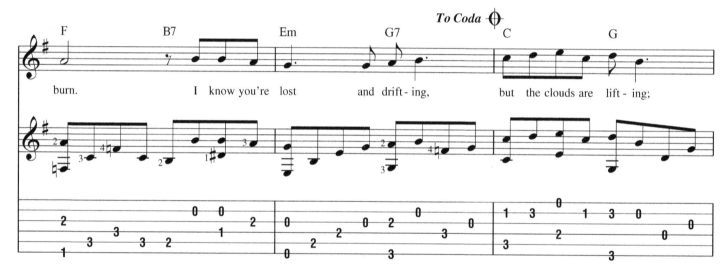

burn.   I know you're lost   and drift-ing,   but the clouds are lift-ing;

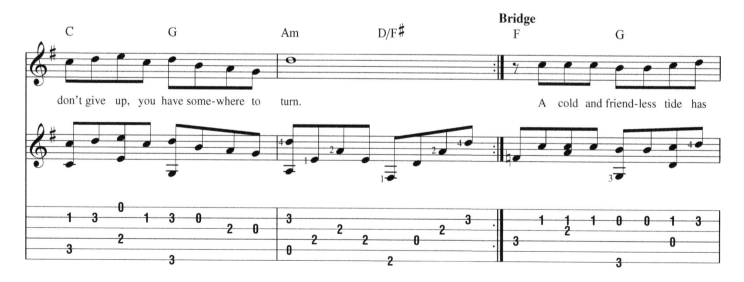

don't give up, you have some-where to   turn.   A cold and friend-less tide has

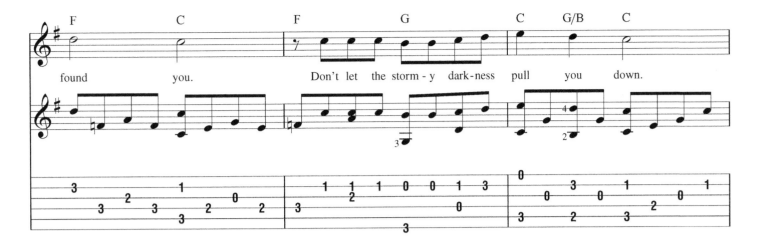

D.C. al Coda

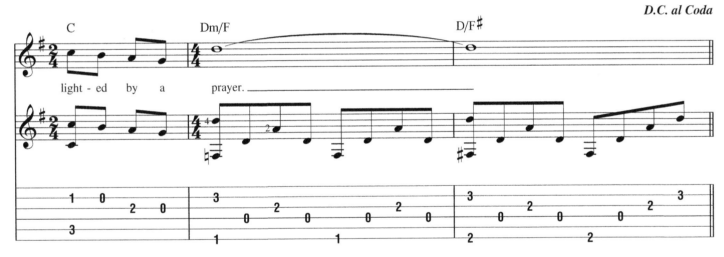

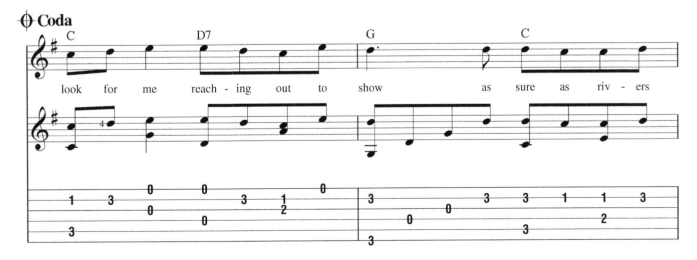

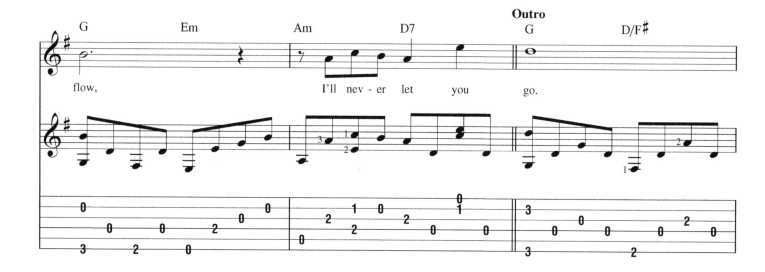

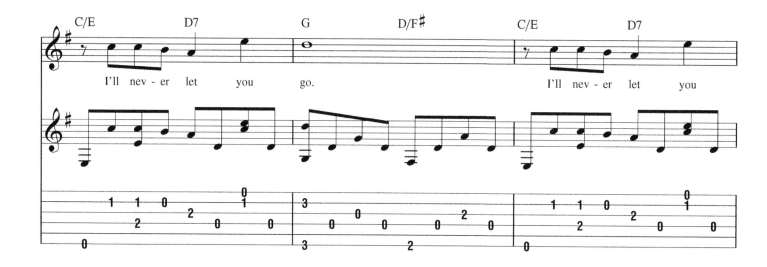

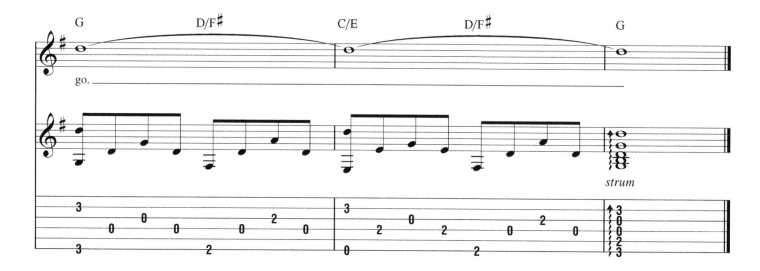

Additional Lyrics

2. I'll be your candle on the water,
   'Til ev'ry wave is warm and bright.
   My soul is there beside you,
   Let this candle guide you;
   Soon you'll see a golden stream of light.

3. I'll be your candle on the water,
   This flame inside of me will grow.
   Keep holding on, you'll make it,
   Here's my hand so take it;
   Look for me reaching out to show
   As sure as rivers flow,
   I'll never let you go.

Colors of the Wind

from Walt Disney's POCAHONTAS

Music by Alan Menken
Lyrics by Stephen Schwartz

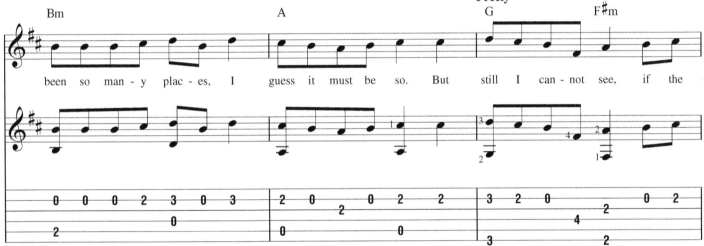

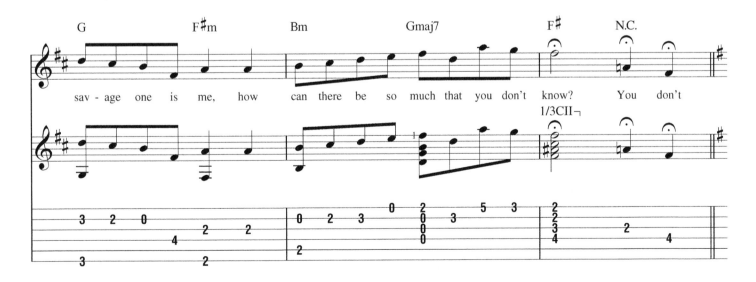

Moderately

know...

§ **Verse**

1. You think you own what-ev-er land you land on; the
2., 3., 4. *See additional lyrics*

earth is just a dead thing you can claim; but I know ev-'ry rock and tree and

4th time, To Coda

crea-ture has a life, has a spir-it, has a name. 2. You

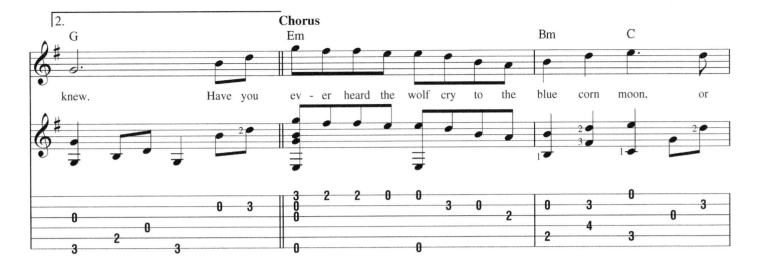

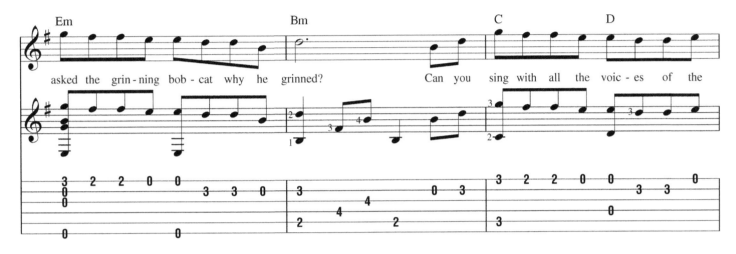

D.S. al Coda
(take reapeat)

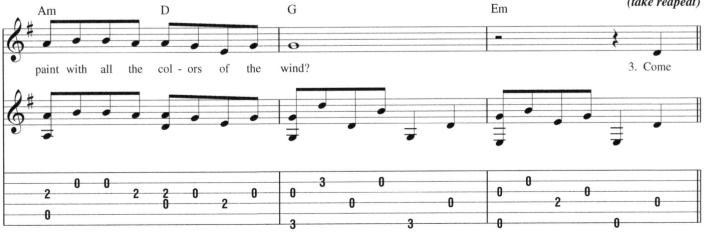

Coda

Bridge

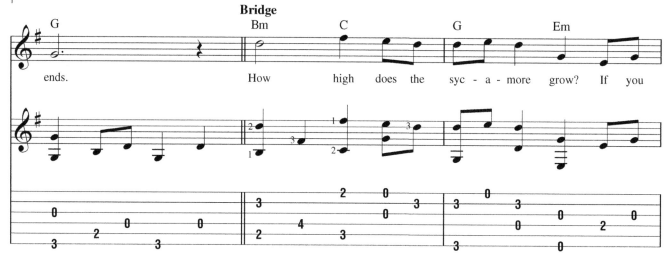

ends.   How   high   does   the   syc - a - more   grow?   If   you

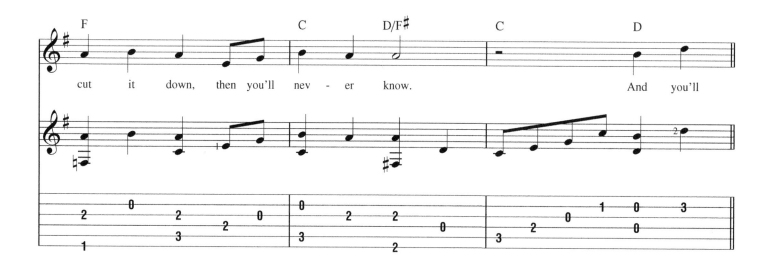

cut   it   down,   then   you'll   nev - er   know.   And   you'll

Chorus

nev - er   hear   the   wolf   cry   to   the   blue   corn   moon,   for   wheth - er   we   are   white   or   cop - per -

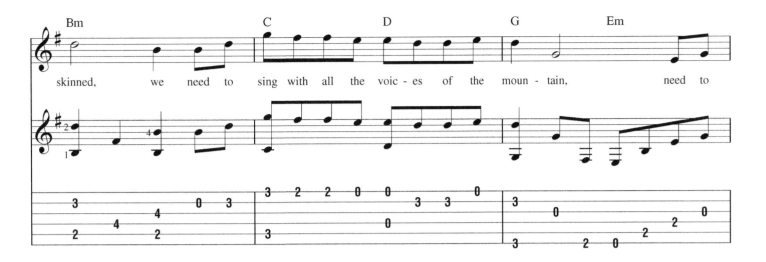

skinned, we need to sing with all the voic-es of the moun - tain, need to

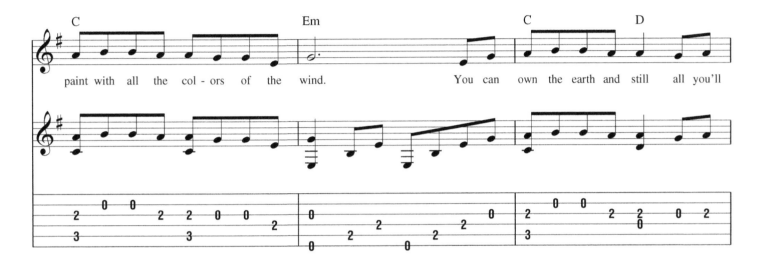

paint with all the col-ors of the wind. You can own the earth and still all you'll

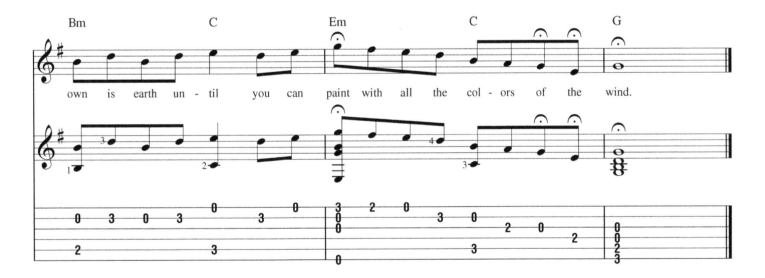

own is earth un - til you can paint with all the col - ors of the wind.

Additional Lyrics

2. You think the only people who are people
   Are the people who look and think like you,
   But if you walk the footsteps of a stranger
   You'll learn things you never knew you never knew.

3. Come run the hidden pine trails of the forest,
   Come taste the sunsweet berries of the earth;
   Come roll in all the riches all around you,
   And for once, never wonder what they're worth.

4. The rainstorm and the river are my brothers;
   The heron and the otter are my friends;
   And we are all connected to each other
   In a circle, in a hoop that never ends.

Go the Distance

from Walt Disney Pictures' HERCULES

Music by Alan Menken
Lyrics by David Zippel

find my way. I can go ___ the dis-tance. I'll be there some - day

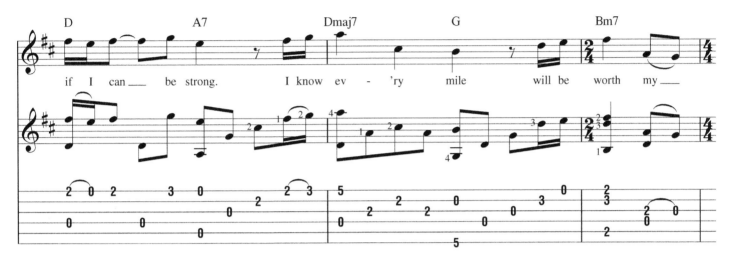

if I can ___ be strong. I know ev - 'ry mile will be worth my ___

while. I would go most an-y-where to feel like

Outro

I _____ be - long. I am on my way.

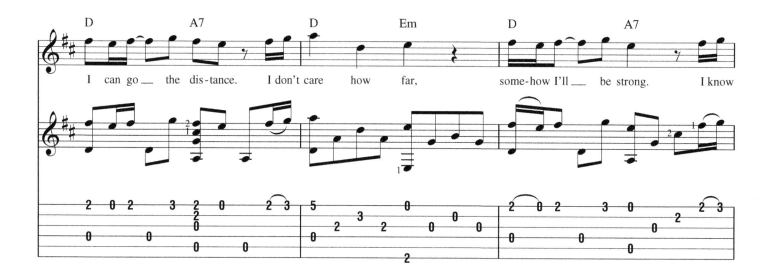

I can go ___ the dis-tance. I don't care how far, some-how I'll ___ be strong. I know

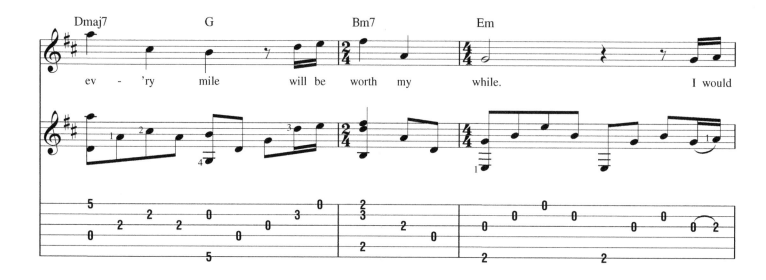

ev - 'ry mile will be worth my while. I would

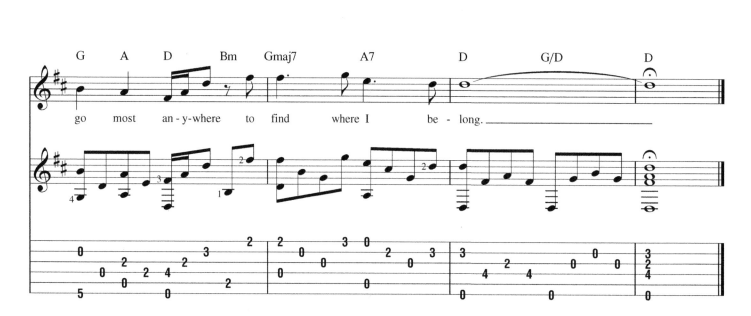

go most an - y-where to find where I be - long. ___

If I Didn't Have You

Walt Disney Pictures Presents A Pixar Animation Studios Film MONSTERS, INC.

Music and Lyrics by Randy Newman

*T=Thumb on 6th string. (Or barre chord.)

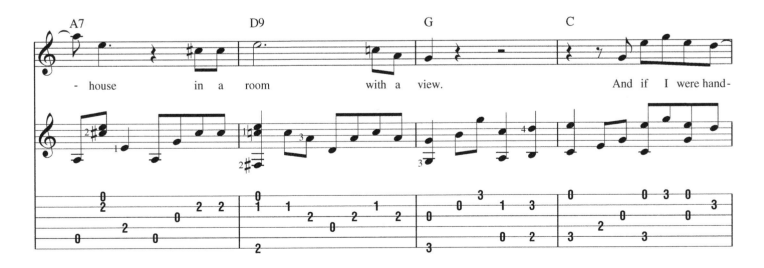

- some   'cause dreams can come true,   I would-n't have

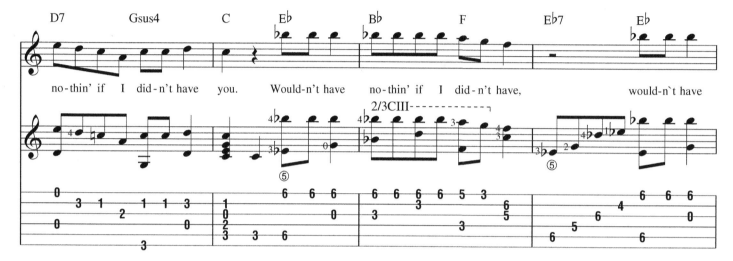

no-thin' if I did-n't have   you.   Would-n't have   no-thin' if I did-n't have,   would-n`t have

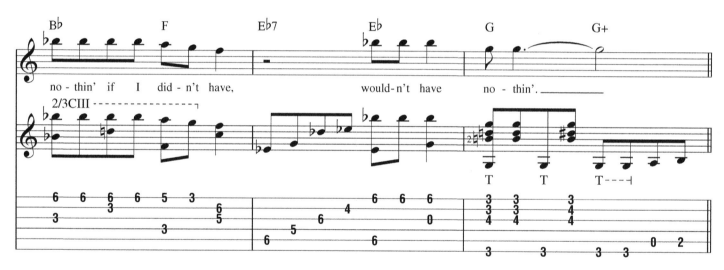

no - thin' if I did -n't have,   would-n't have   no - thin'. _____

Verse

2. For years I have en - vied   your grace and your charm. _

Ev-'ry-one loves _ you, _____ you know. _____ Yes, I know, I know, _ I know.

But I must ad - mit it, big guy, you al - ways come through.

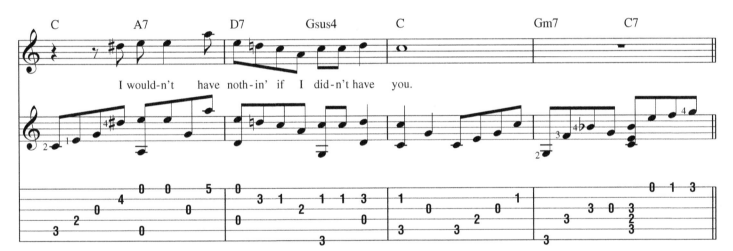

I would-n't have noth-in' if I did-n't have you.

Bridge

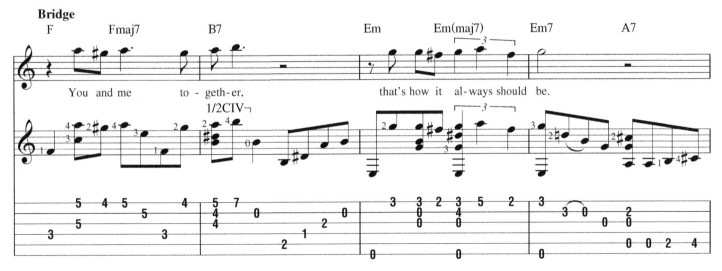

You and me to - geth-er, that's how it al - ways should be.

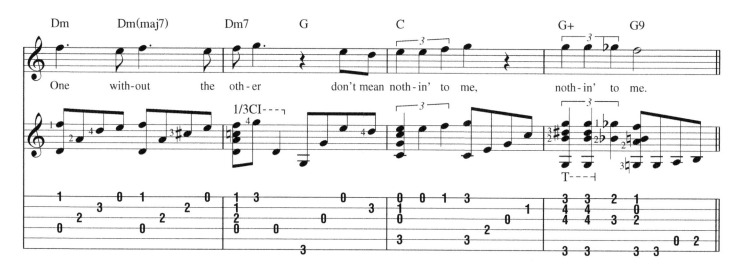

One with-out the oth-er don't mean noth-in' to me, noth-in' to me.

Outro-Verse

Yes, I would-n't be noth-in' if I did-n't have you.

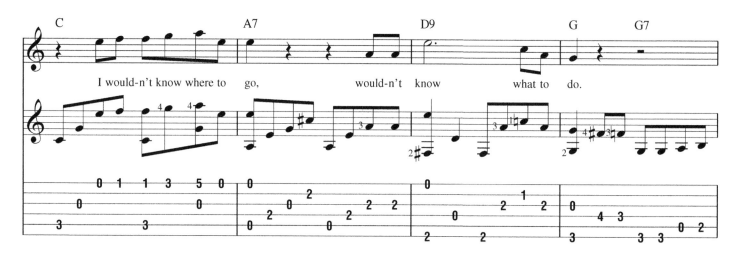

I would-n't know where to go, would-n't know what to do.

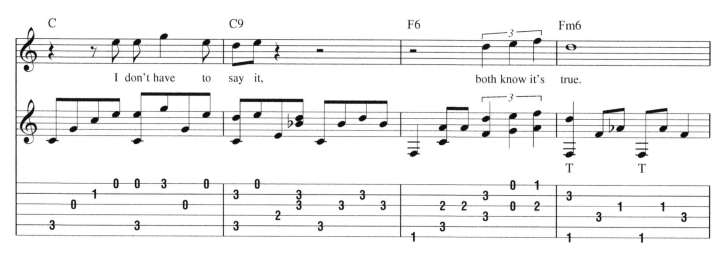

I don't have to say it, both know it's true.

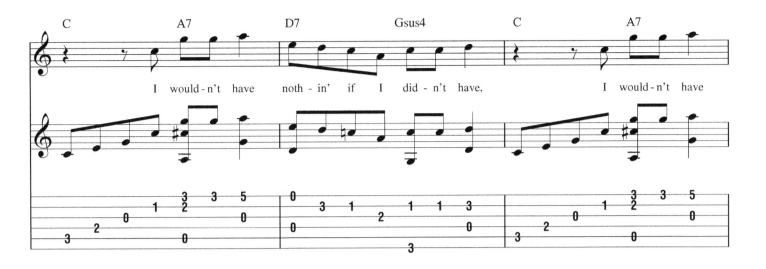

I would-n't have noth-in' if I did-n't have, I would-n't have

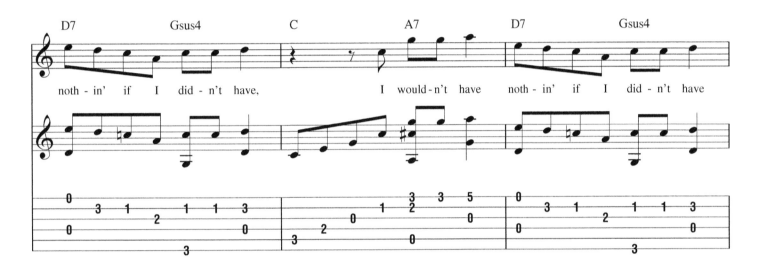

noth-in' if I did-n't have, I would-n't have noth-in' if I did-n't have

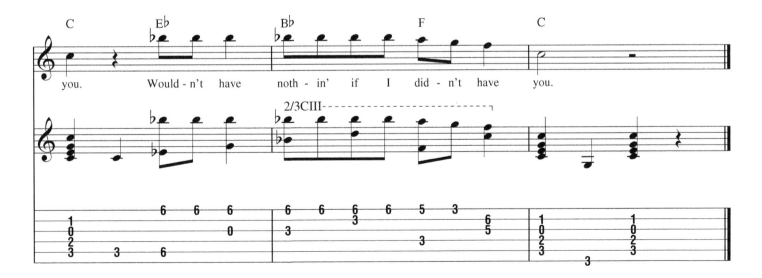

you. Would-n't have noth-in' if I did-n't have you.

Look Through My Eyes

from Walt Disney Pictures' BROTHER BEAR

Words and Music by Phil Collins

1. There are things in ___ life you'll
2. *See additional lyrics*

learn and ___ oh, in time you'll ___ see, ___

'cause out there some - where __ it's all wait - ing __ if you

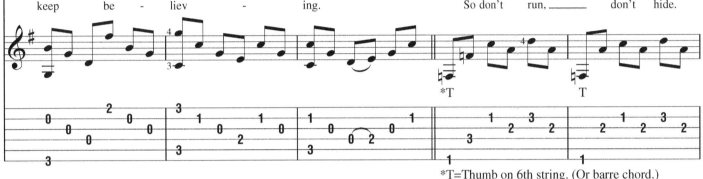

Pre-Chorus

keep be - liev - ing. So don't run, _____ don't hide.

*T=Thumb on 6th string. (Or barre chord.)

It will be al - right. You'll see; _____ trust me. _____ I'll be

𝄋 Chorus

there _____ watch-ing o - ver you. Just take a look through __ my __

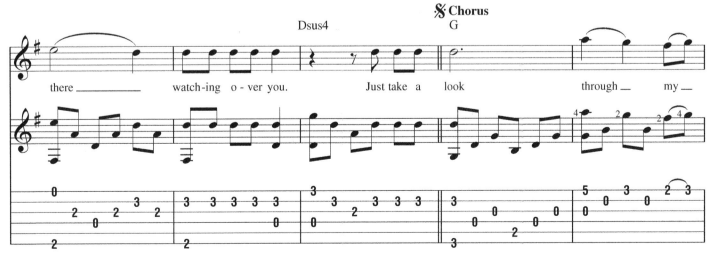

33

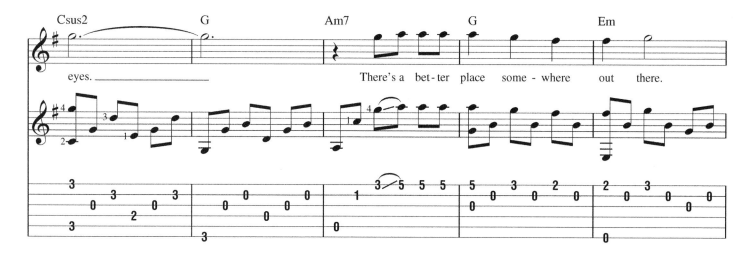

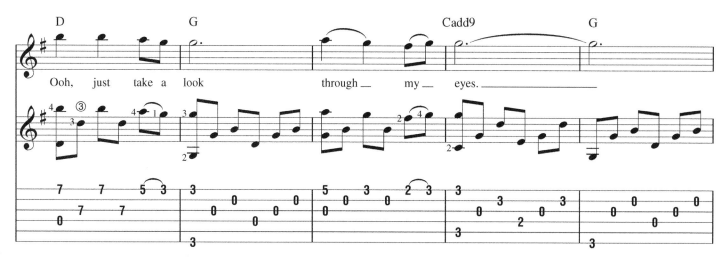

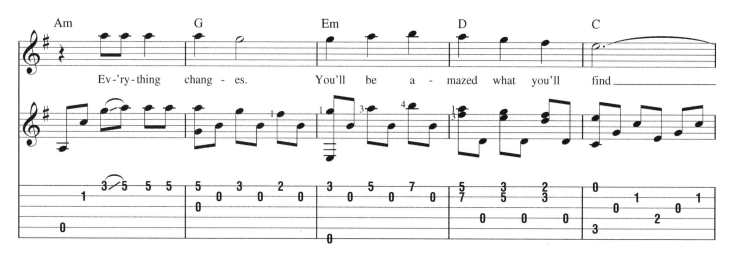

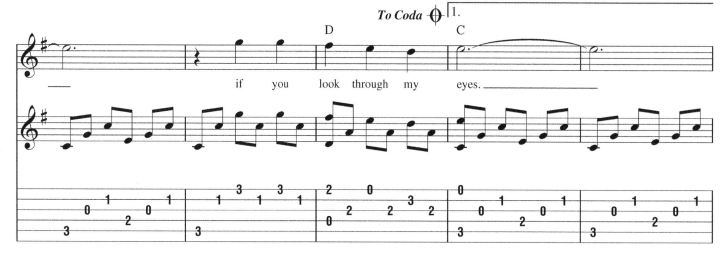

 **Coda**

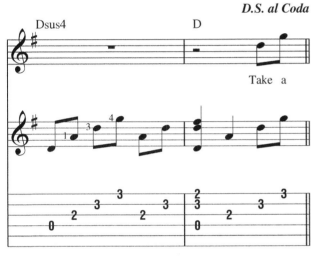

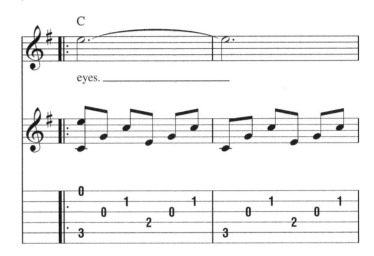

Additional Lyrics

2. There will be times on this journey,
   All you see is darkness,
   But out there somewhere daylight finds you
   If you keep believing.

My Funny Friend and Me

from Walt Disney Pictures' THE EMPEROR'S NEW GROOVE

Lyrics by Sting
Music by Sting and David Hartley

Drop D tuning:
(low to high) D–A–D–G–B–E

Slowly

In the qui - et time of eve - ning, when the stars as-sume their

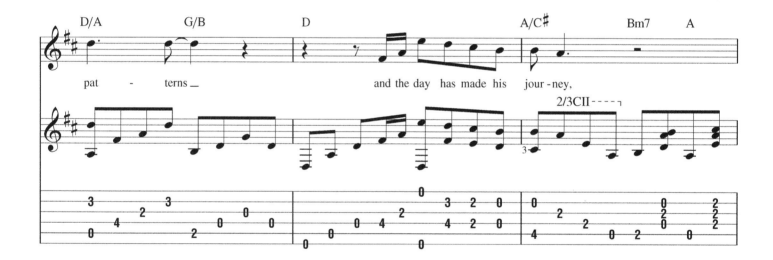

pat - terns _ and the day has made his jour-ney,

and we won-der just what hap - pened to the life we knew, be-fore the

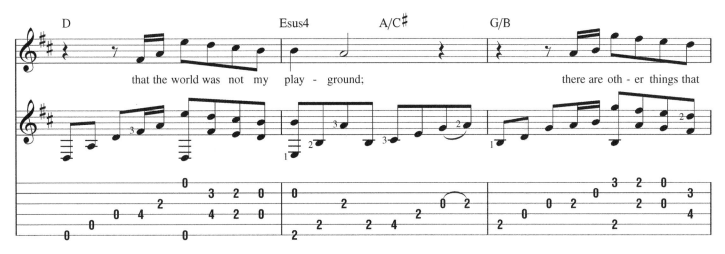

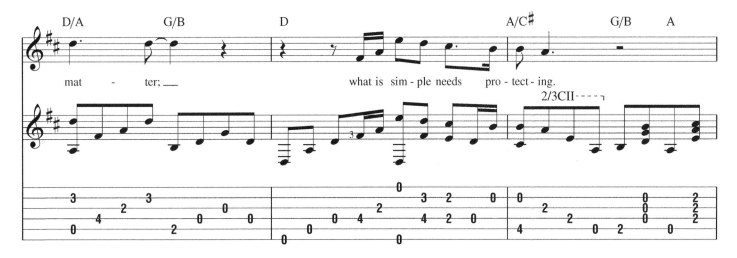

those con - stel - la - tions look like you and I. ___ Just like the pat - terns in the

big sky, ___ we could be lost; we could re - fuse to try. But to have

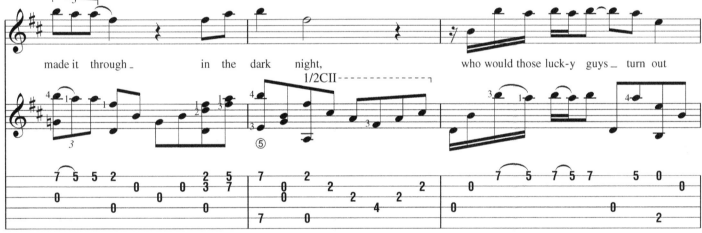

made it through ___ in the dark night, who would those luck-y guys ___ turn out

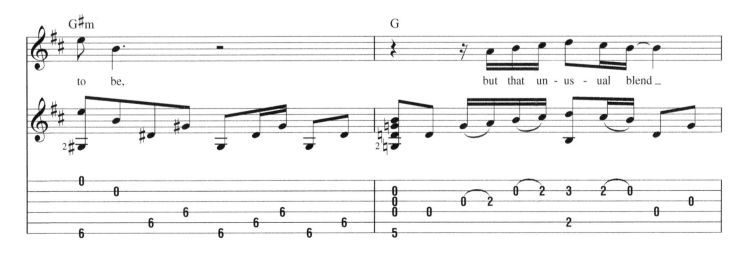

to be, but that un - us - ual blend ___

of my fun-ny friend and me.

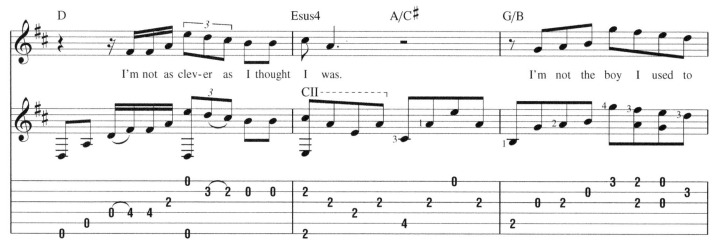

I'm not as clev-er as I thought I was.   I'm not the boy I used to

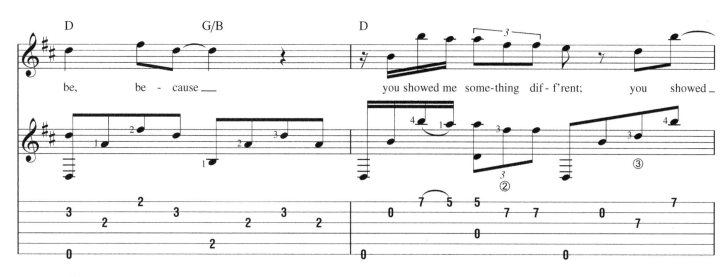

be,   be - cause ___   you showed me some-thing dif - f'rent;   you showed ___

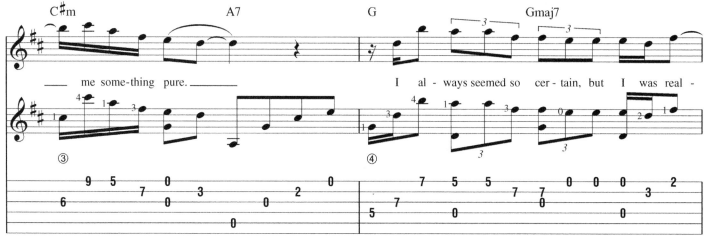

___ me some-thing pure. ___   I al - ways seemed so cer - tain, but I was real -

Reflection

from Walt Disney Pictures' MULAN

Music by Matthew Wilder
Lyrics by David Zippel

Drop D tuning:
(low to high) D–A–D–G–B–E

Verse
Moderately slow

1. Look at me, you may think you see ___ who I ___ real - ly am, ___ but you'll nev - er know me. Ev - 'ry day, it's as if I play ___ a

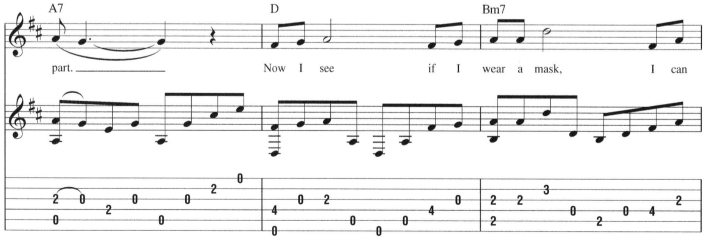

part. _____ Now I see if I wear a mask, I can

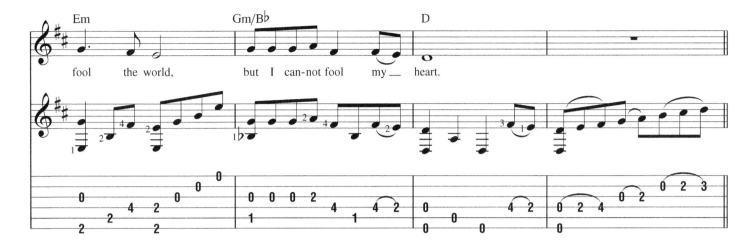

fool the world, but I can-not fool my ___ heart.

Chorus

Who is that girl I see ___ star- ing straight ___

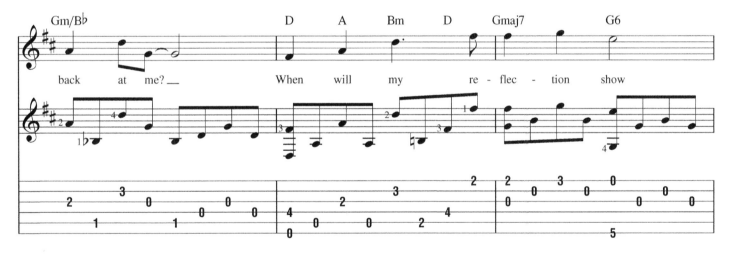

back at me? ___ When will my re - flec - tion show

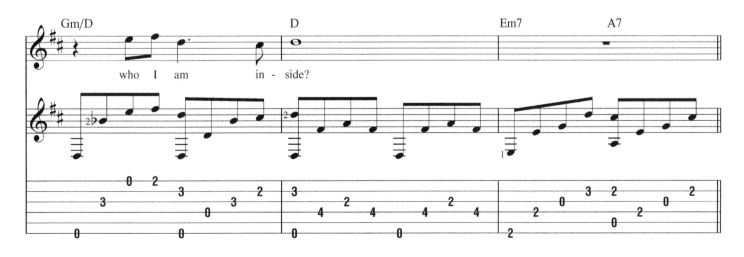

who I am in - side?

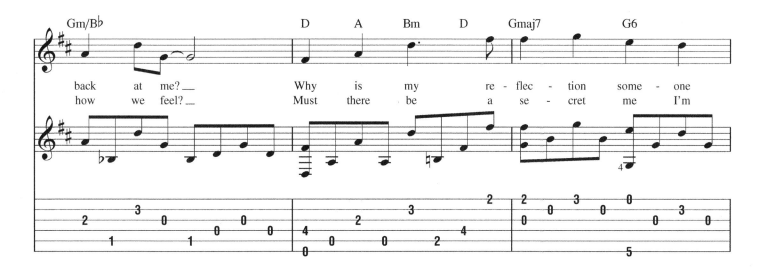

back at me? ___ Why is my re - flec - tion some - one
how we feel? ___ Must there be a se - cret me I'm

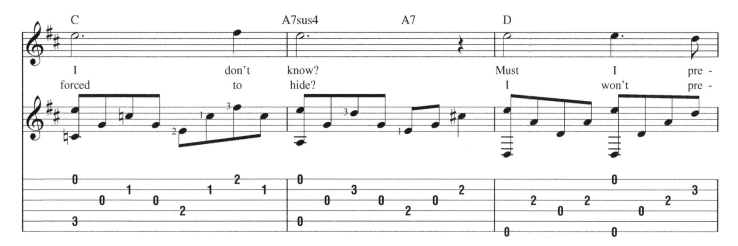

I don't know?
forced to hide?
Must I won't pre - pre -

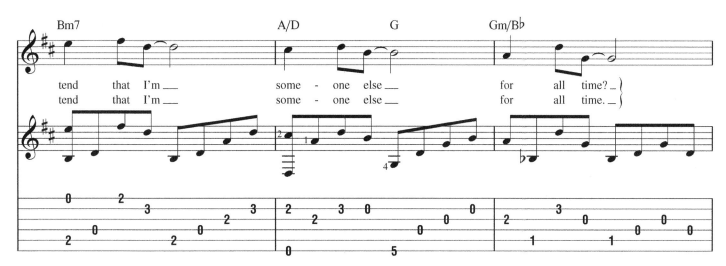

tend that I'm ___ some - one else ___ for all time? ___
tend that I'm ___ some - one else ___ for all time. ___

To Coda ⊕

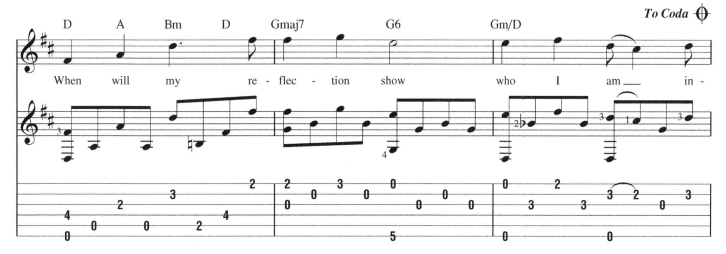

When will my re - flec - tion show who I am ___ in -

Bridge

side? ___ There's a heart that must be free to fly, that

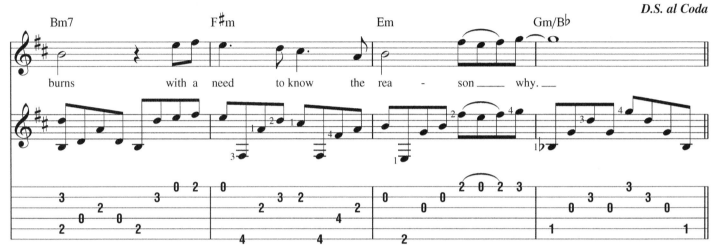

D.S. al Coda

burns with a need to know the rea - son ___ why. ___

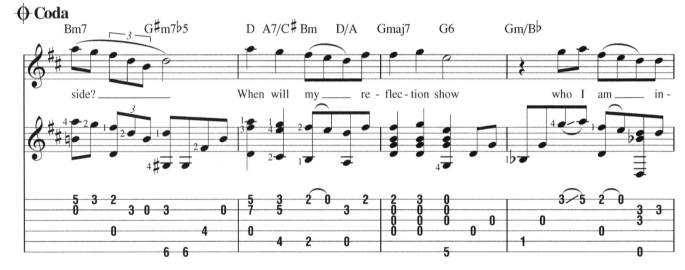

⊕ Coda

side? ___ When will my ___ re - flec - tion show who I am ___ in-

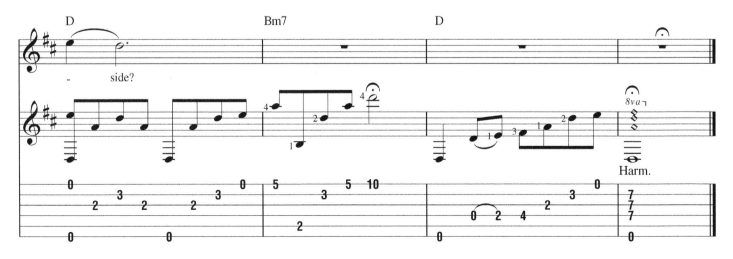

- side?

A Whole New World

from Walt Disney's ALADDIN

Music by Alan Menken
Lyrics by Tim Rice

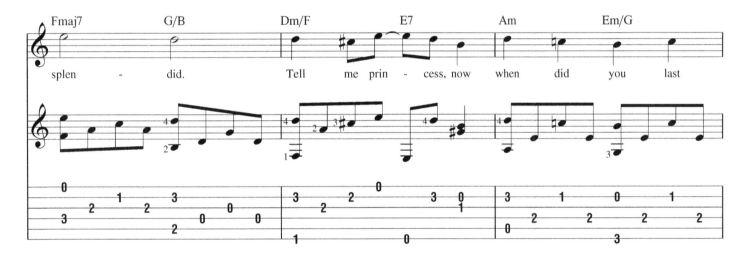

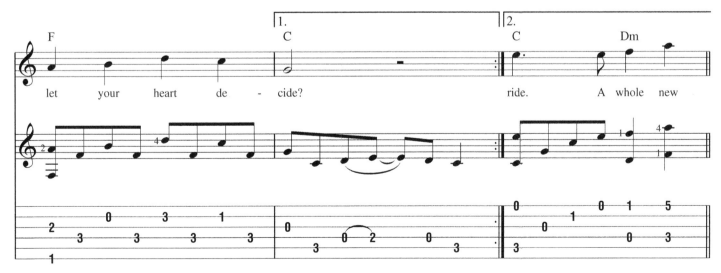

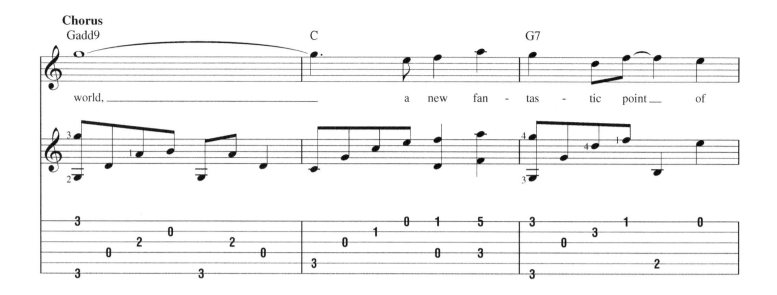

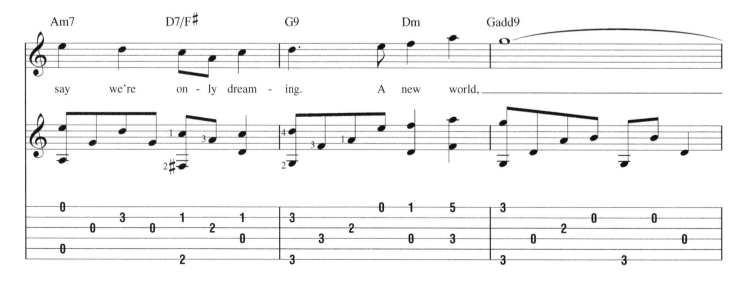

a daz - zling place I nev - er knew. But, when I'm way up here, it's

cry - stal clear that now I'm in a whole new world with you.

Additional Lyrics

2. I can open your eyes,
Take you wonder by wonder,
Over, sideways and under,
On a magic carpet ride.

Under the Sea

from Walt Disney's THE LITTLE MERMAID

Lyrics by Howard Ashman
Music by Alan Menken

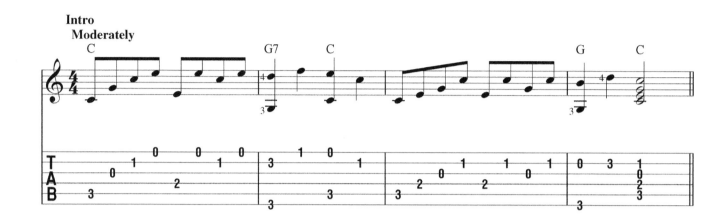

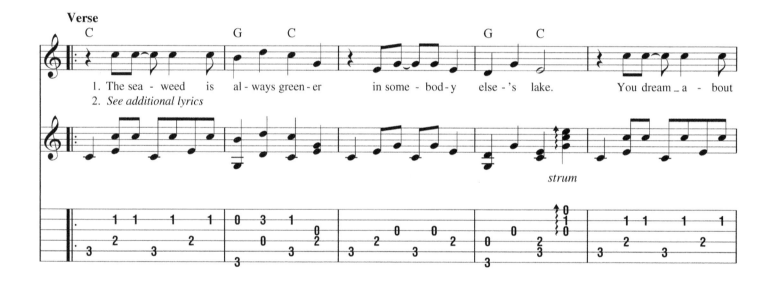

Chorus

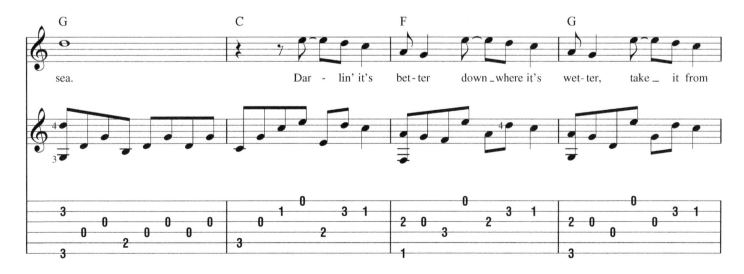

me.   Up __ on the   shore they work __ all day.   Out __ in the

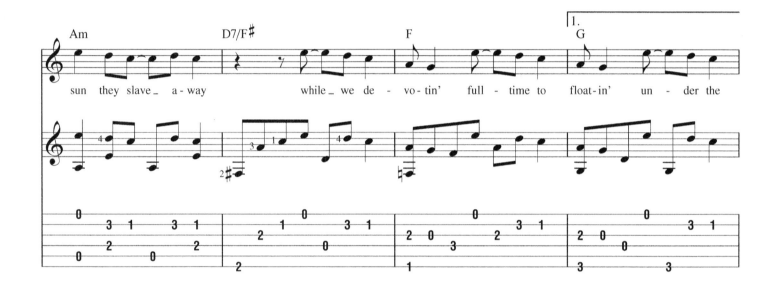

sun they slave __ a - way   while __ we de - vo - tin'   full - time to   float-in'   un - der the

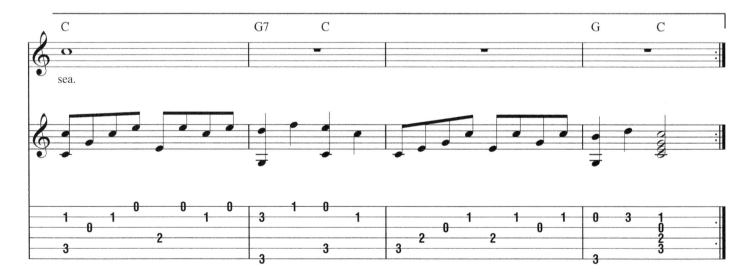

sea.

52

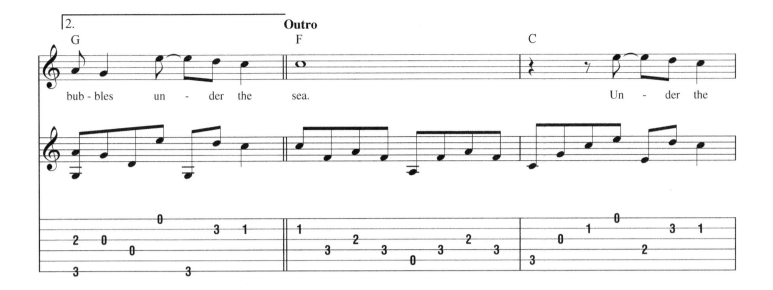

bub - bles   un - der the   sea.   Un - der the

sea.   Since _ life is   sweet here,   we _ got the   beat here   nat - u - ral -

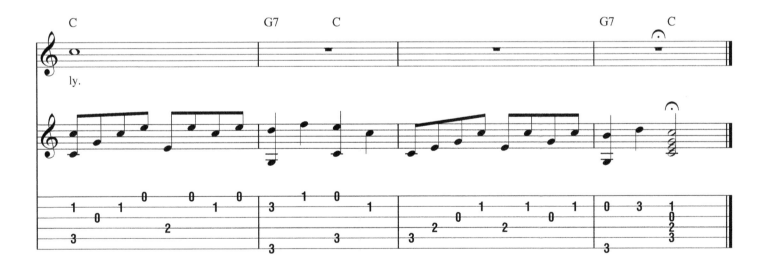

ly.

Additional Lyrics

2. Down here all the fish is happy
   As off through the waves dey roll.
   The fish on the land ain't happy,
   They sad 'cause they in the bowl.
   But fish in the bowl is lucky,
   They in for a worser fate.
   One day when the boss get hungry,
   Guess who's gon' be on the plate?

Chorus Under the sea, under the sea.
   Nobody beat us, fry us, and eat us in fricasee.
   We what the land folks loves to cook,
   Under the sea we off the hook.
   We got no troubles, life is the bubbles under the sea.
   Under the sea.
   Since life is sweet here, we got the beat here naturally.

You'll Be in My Heart
(Pop Version)
from Walt Disney Pictures' TARZAN™
Words and Music by Phil Collins

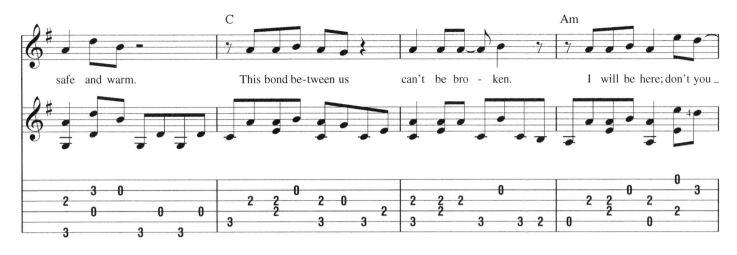

safe and warm. This bond be-tween us can't be bro - ken. I will be here; don't you _

Chorus

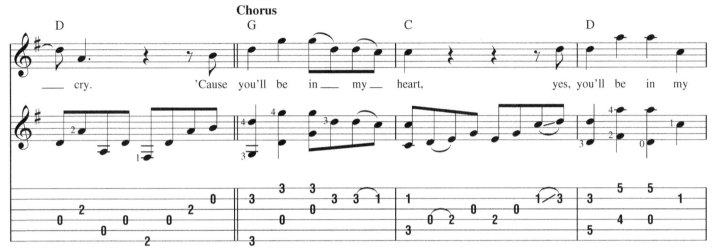

_ cry. 'Cause you'll be in _ my _ heart, yes, you'll be in my

To Coda ⊕

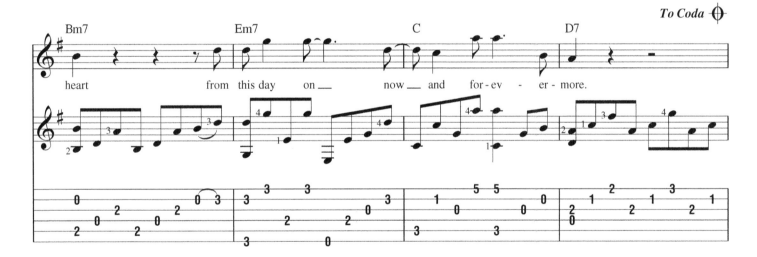

heart from this day on _ now _ and for - ev - er - more.

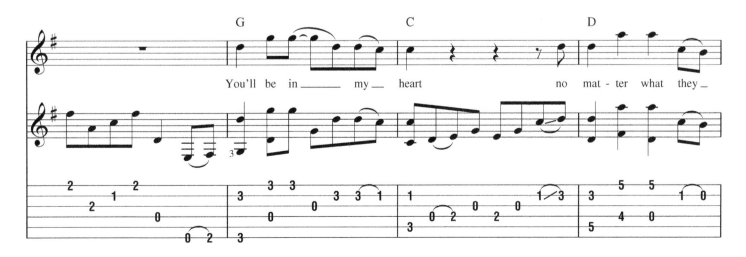

You'll be in _ my _ heart no mat - ter what they _

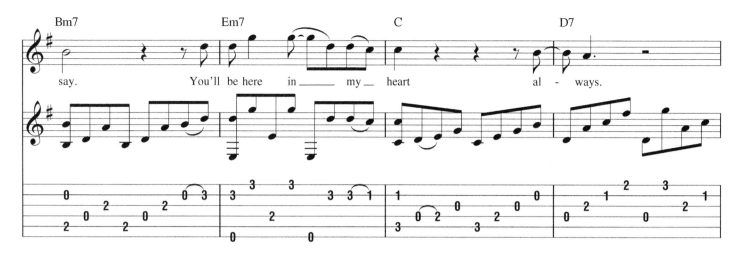

say.　You'll be here in ____ my ___ heart　al - ways.

Coda

D.S. al Coda

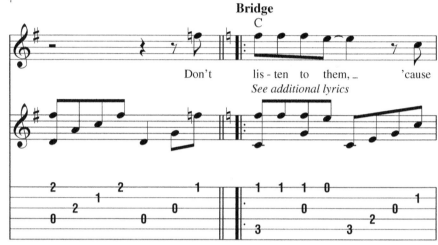

Bridge

C

Don't　lis - ten to them, _ 'cause

See additional lyrics

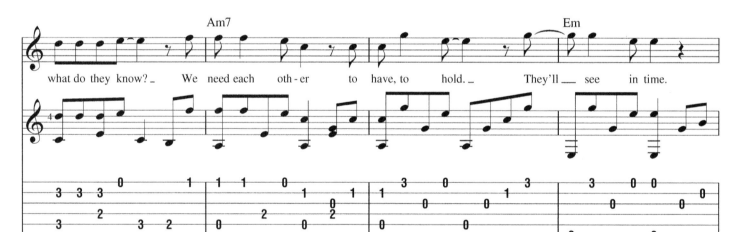

Am7　　　　　　　　　　　　　　　　　　　　Em

what do they know? _ We need each oth - er　to have, to　hold. _　They'll __ see　in time.

1.
Fmaj7

I ____ know. _

2.
Fmaj7

When __ know. _　We'll

Outro-Chorus

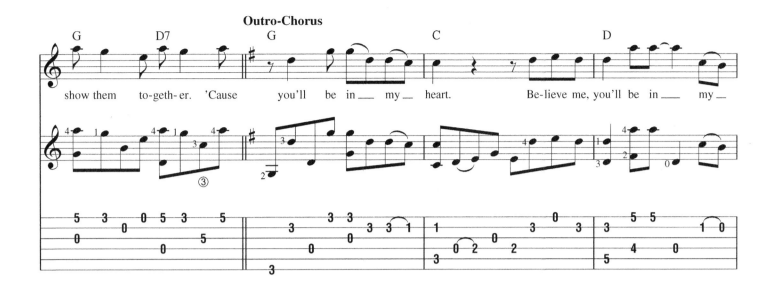

show them to-geth-er. 'Cause you'll be in my heart. Be-lieve me, you'll be in my

heart. I'll be there from this day on, now and for-ev-er-more.

You'll be in my heart no mat-ter what they

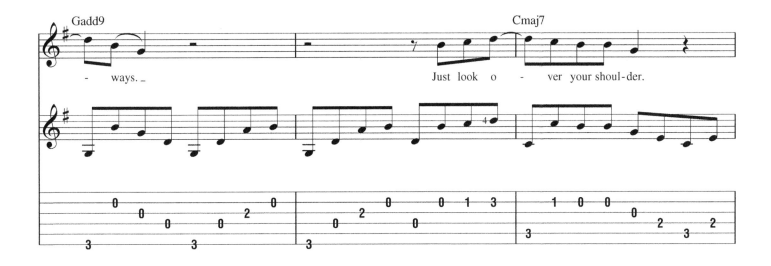

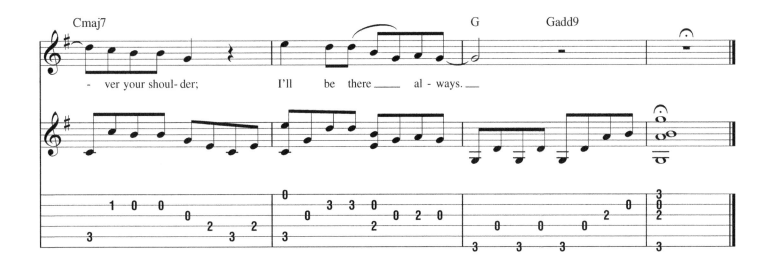

Additional Lyrics

2. Why can't they understand the way we feel?
They just don't trust what they can't explain.
I know we're diff'rent but deep inside us
We're not that different at all.
And you'll be in my heart...

Bridge When destiny calls you, you must be strong.
I may not be with you, but you've got to hold on.
They'll see in time, I know.

You've Got a Friend in Me

from Walt Disney's TOY STORY

Music and Lyrics by Randy Newman

Intro
Moderately

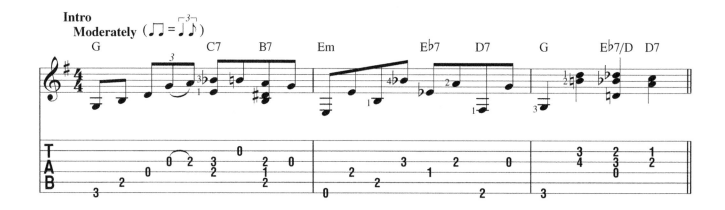

Verse

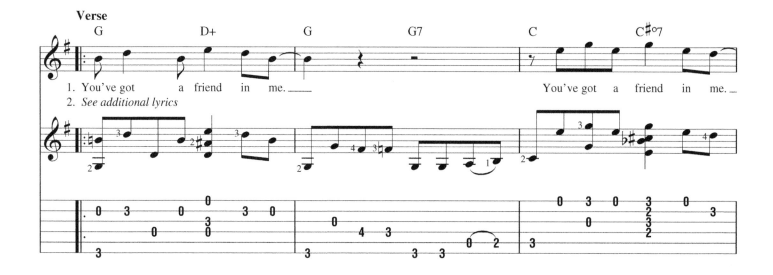

1. You've got a friend in me. ___ You've got a friend in me. ___
2. *See additional lyrics*

___ When the road ___ looks rough a - head ___ and you're miles ___

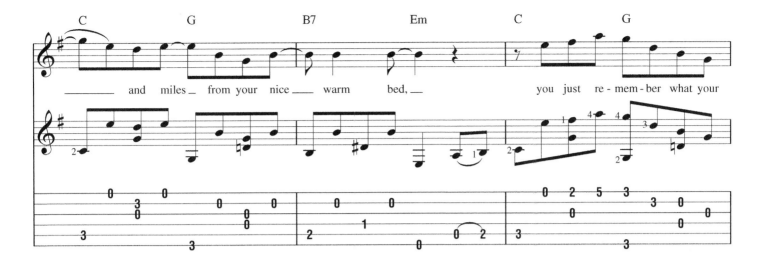

and miles from your nice warm bed, you just re - mem - ber what your

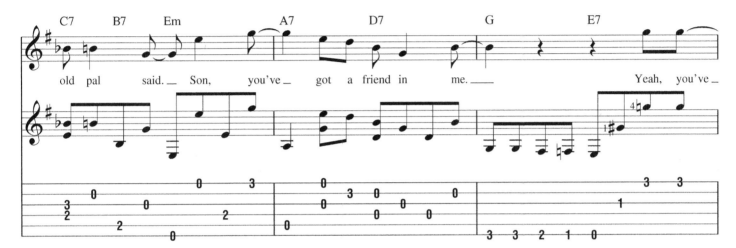

old pal said. Son, you've got a friend in me. Yeah, you've

1.

got a friend in me.

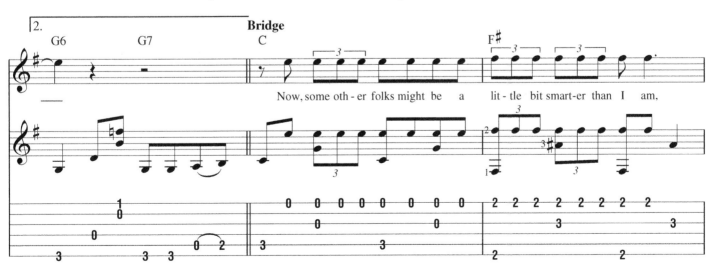

2. **Bridge**

Now, some oth - er folks might be a lit - tle bit smart - er than I am,

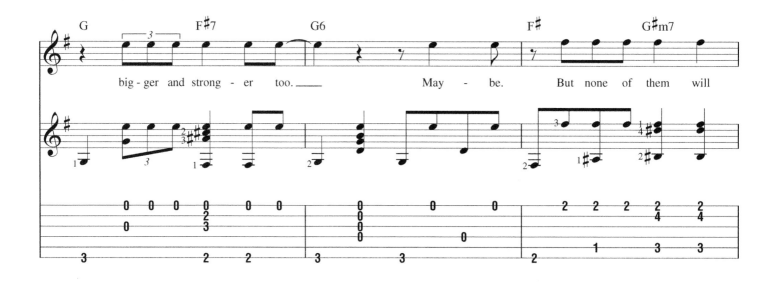

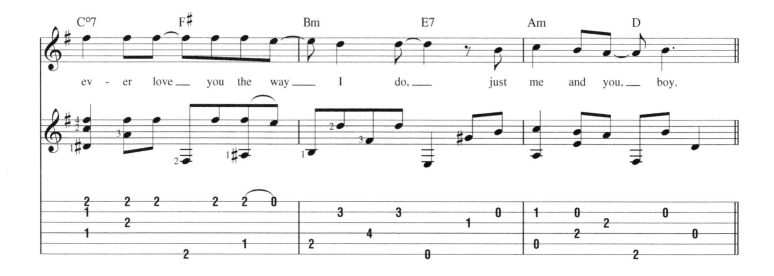

Outro-Verse

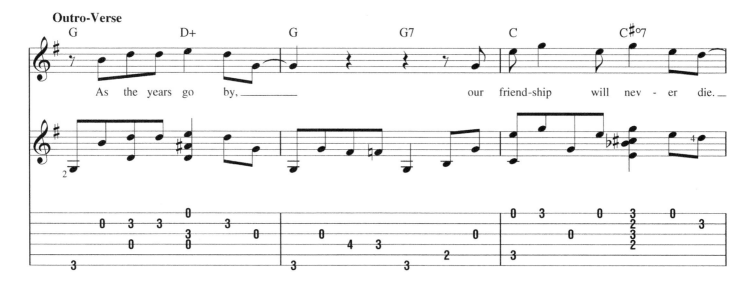

You're gon - na   see   it's our des - ti - ny.   You've got a friend in   me. _

You've got a friend in   me. _   You've got a friend in me. _

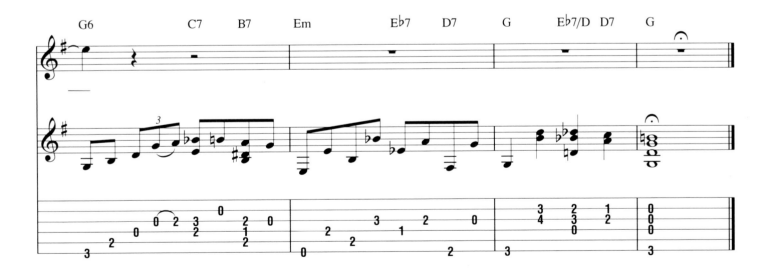

Additional Lyrics

2. You've got a friend in me.
   You've got a friend in me.
   You got troubles, then I got 'em too.
   There isn't anything I wouldn't do for you.
   If we stick together we can see it through.
   'Cause you've got a friend in me.
   Yeah, you've got a friend in me.